Looky Loo

Makala Pekos

BookLeaf Publishing

Looky Loo © 2022 Makala Pekos

All rights reserved.

No part of this publication may be reproduced, stored in a retrieval system, or transmitted, in any form or by any means, electronic, mechanical, photocopying, recording or otherwise, without the prior written permission of the presenters.

Makala Pekos asserts the moral right to be identified as author of this work.

Presentation by *BookLeaf Publishing*

Web: www.bookleafpub.com

E-mail: info@bookleafpub.com

ISBN: 9789395756617

First edition 2022

ACKNOWLEDGEMENT

Please check out my poetry on
poeticplaguedoctor.com

PREFACE

A good poem is like a train wreck, you just can't look away.

Step Off

Forgive me and I will do the same,
repudiate me and I'm free from blame.
Though I will not tax my memory,
by cataloging all you've done to me.
Eventually the camels back will break,
for there's only so one person can take.
So please, remember the Golden Rule,
and stop treating me as your foot stool.

You Done Did It

Smack you in the face like a flag caught by wind
the truth never hurts so bad like when you know
you've sinned
wishing you could undo it all, your pennies keep
hitting the floor
if only you hadn't opened your mouth or ever
left the door
but you did and you did and there's no going
back
your only hope is to grovel and grope
and pray they show the self-control you lack

Here's a Toast

Drink to sun
Drink to life
Drink to having
no worries or strife

Drink for happy
and..to days pass
to my lovey..famly
to hope it will last

Drink times..when are hard
all when and is...smooth
Drink trying...forget to...when
or to you've...something...prove

Medicine

Numb, numb
My tongues turned dumb
My hearts turned to stone but the pain isn't gone

I've tried to fight it
Now I throw down my arms
My efforts do no good and do much harm

Reflection

What do I see when I look in the mirror?
Someone who needs sleep.
A strong person, who works well in a crisis,
and not afraid to openly weep.
What do you see when you look at me?
Because of many things it differs.
My mood, time day, and most importantly,
and what you see in the your mirror.

WHAT DID YOU SAY?!

Hello
I'm a person
You may say no but it's true

Yes I can feel
Though I know it won't change what you do

Treat me like a doormat or a bug to be squashed,
it may hurt me or no either way it's your loss.

Because I am a person,
And I will not be broken
Not by any action taken
Nor any word spoken

Shadows

Their Empty
they feed off my fear
my screams are like music
the finest of wines are my tears

How can you fight what isn't really there?
Do you yell at the wind?
Or beat the air?

Its all in my head, I know that much at least
But does that make it any better?
Now its beyond reach!

No one can touch them!
No one can help!
I'm all on my own!
All by myself...

Sunset Sonata

As the day comes to an end
a rythym fills my heart
the grandest of processions
is just about to start

The colors at first are muted
light oranges and soft pinks
they dance across the sky
as the sun begins to sink

The clouds along the horizon
are then set ablaze in the sky
purples splash, oranges now smolder
and sparks of yellow fly

The sun nearly gone, but the show isn't over
its only intermission
for as the sapphire sea rolls over the sky
the dancers take their positions

They merrily dance their moonlight ballet
waving goodbye to the sun
and as the lead performer takes her place
the sunset sonata is done

Someday

The lights, the crowd
The clamourous applause
For many this is the end all of living

They starve, they lie, they sell themselves out
Soon don't recognize themselves in the mirror

Reach for it, starving model
Reach for it, haggard singer
Reach for it, impoverished actor

Someday the crowd my chant your name
Someday you may reach worldwide acclaim
Someday you may be the pinnacle of fame

Possibly, maybe, someday

Drop in the Cup

I was tired and you cooked for me
Drop in the cup
My legs gave out and you carried me
Drop in the cup
My shoulders dislocated and you helped me put the right
Drop in the cup
When my migraine was bad you went without light
Drop in the cup
I was born, like many, with a cup bone dry and many problems to keep it so
But you singlehandedly have filled my cups so high, to the point where it overflows

Dirge of the Reserved

Writing comes easy
It's speaking that's so hard
Whenever I try to converse
I just seem to fall apart

I want to be the person
People flock to for a chat
But as it is I'm the person
No one notices in the back

I want so much to be vivacious
To laugh aloud without fear
And yet here I am talking stock of the world
And writing so no one will hear

Untitled

As I lay here in my bed staring at the white ceiling above
My mind keeping me awake with every failure it can think of
I wonder what will happen to me, whats life got in store
I here noises that make me jump, I 'm afraid. But fear is my poison.
I drink it everyday, will I ever build up a tolerance? I wonder when this will all be over.
It might be only the start. But I wish I knew something of my own condition
...or maybe just a part. But no. I'm in the dark.
Just like this room I'm lying in, its enveloping, I can't see past.
My eyes desperately searching for a glimmer, just a shimmer.
But not one made it through. So I take a deep breath and close my eyes altogether,
and imagine myself far away. My body relaxes, the darkness soon passes, and soon comes break of day.

R.M.P. Remember Me Please

The world goes by
you live you die
the world moves on
your here your gone

oh how fleeting these moments are
flickering like firebugs in a jar
we try to stop the flow of time
with creams and lotions and exercise
but even before our time is up
unnatural death can always come

People look on
and can only cry
as all their loved ones
say goodbye

Today your leaving the womb of your mother
tomorrow your buried six feet under
and some even have a different tomb
never leaving their mothers womb
until the time when this system ends
death comes to all, for all have sinned

The soul leaves

then you rot or burn
"from dust you are
to dust you shall return"

Knowing and Doing

Round and round and round I go
Vascilating within myself
As I war with the monster raging inside
I take it out on everyone else.
I become a walking bomb that can go off at anytime
and everyone around me knows it.
So they run and avoid me,
and duck away and hide.

And then I wonder why I'm so lonely...

Life on the Road

Grass just rushes by,
Blurs of emerald under a sapphire sky.
The trees, tall giants, sway in the breeze.
Changing from magnolias to evergreens.

The asphalt webs that span the nation,
Make for a quick and carefree vacation.
And family bonds made on a trip,
Cannot be broken, not one bit.

These are the moments that we'll remember,
In the days of life's December.
On the open road, with laughs and tears
What we'll call the Golden years

Try to Laugh When You Want to Cry

Try to laugh when you want to cry
Feel like a liar Everytime you smile
Don't even know why I feel this way
I'm so lonely inside
But I want everyone to go away
I can't stand my own reflection
Everything about myself makes me sick
I don't know what to do
Or how I got like this

Meh

Livings such a bore
a chore
a never ending drain on my soul
my brain
end it all
end the pain
easy way out
would anyone blame?
I'm tired
who isn't?
Is that even a reason?
I hurt
Who doesn't?
Just because I can't see them
I'm tired of being lonely
But I know it's all my fault
I cry, I moan
no wonder they don't draw close
they have enough of their own

I'm Just So Hungry!!

I hunger for a day without pain
a time when this Earths rain
would be life sustaining,
free from acid and dirt.
I hunger for a day
when war will be gone,
gone like the so many fallen by its
scarred and marred history.
I hunger for a time when life
will be made new, fresh like the dew
on a summers day.
I hunger for sickness to be a memory,
and anger to be a thing of the past,
and for Hunger to be no more.

Letter of Recommendation

Don't look back
eyes on the prize
they say its easy
thats nothing but lies
you knew it, you dont care
you were always aware
you took their false words as a dare
transparent and heartless
you knew they were wrong,
it didnt take you long,
it only made you strong

They threw the glove
so you rose above
its not enough for you to simply be good
you strive for nothing less
than the best
wish is why you excell
I wish you well

Let There Be Peace

Let your smile shine for all to see
Let your words be sweet and filled with meaning
Let your eyes always be looking for the brighter side
Let your legs be swift to run from a fight
Let your hands always be working in the interests of another
And let each one treat his neighbor as a dear brother

Listen

I'm so tried in my joints
Sore in my very marrow
Everywhere I look there's no shouts of joy
Only mournful cries of sorrow

CPSIA information can be obtained
at www.ICGtesting.com
Printed in the USA
BVHW050900140623
665885BV00014B/1319

9 789395 756617